LEADERS LIKE US

Alvin Ailey

BY KAITLYN DULING

ILLUSTRATED BY
ARVILLA MAE MORETT

ROURKE'S
SCHOOL to HOME
CONNECTIONS
BEFORE AND DURING READING ACTIVITIES

Before Reading: *Building Background Knowledge and Vocabulary*

Building background knowledge can help children process new information and build upon what they already know. Before reading a book, it is important to tap into what children already know about the topic. This will help them develop their vocabulary and increase their reading comprehension.

Questions and Activities to Build Background Knowledge:

1. Look at the front cover of the book and read the title. What do you think this book will be about?
2. What do you already know about this topic?
3. Take a book walk and skim the pages. Look at the table of contents, photographs, captions, and bold words. Did these text features give you any information or predictions about what you will read in this book?

Vocabulary: *Vocabulary Is Key to Reading Comprehension*

Use the following directions to prompt a conversation about each word.

- Read the vocabulary words.
- What comes to mind when you see each word?
- What do you think each word means?

> **Vocabulary Words:**
> - *choreographer*
> - *come out*
> - *director*
> - *heritage*
> - *integrated*
> - *LGBTQ*
> - *mentor*
> - *muse*

During Reading: *Reading for Meaning and Understanding*

To achieve deep comprehension of a book, children are encouraged to use close reading strategies. During reading, it is important to have children stop and make connections. These connections result in deeper analysis and understanding of a book.

 Close Reading a Text

During reading, have children stop and talk about the following:

- Any confusing parts
- Any unknown words
- Text to text, text to self, text to world connections
- The main idea in each chapter or heading

Encourage children to use context clues to determine the meaning of any unknown words. These strategies will help children learn to analyze the text more thoroughly as they read.

When you are finished reading this book, turn to the next-to-last page for **Text-Dependent Questions** and an **Extension Activity**.

TABLE OF CONTENTS

DISCOVERING DANCE......................................4

BECOMING A CHOREOGRAPHER 6

STEPPING INTO THE SPOTLIGHT 16

TIME LINE 21

GLOSSARY 22

INDEX...23

TEXT-DEPENDENT QUESTIONS.....................23

EXTENSION ACTIVITY................................23

ABOUT THE AUTHOR
AND ILLUSTRATOR 24

DISCOVERING DANCE

Do you ever get the itch to jump up and dance? Have you ever tried to express yourself or tell a story through dance moves? Alvin Ailey knew that movement and dance were very powerful things.

The stage was dark at first. Audience members murmured and waited. In the wings, the dancers got ready. Alvin was the **choreographer**. He listened for the music. It was almost time! Alvin believed that dance was for *everybody*. He was going to lead the way. He was going to tell important stories through dance.

BECOMING A CHOREOGRAPHER

Alvin was born in 1931. He lived with his mom in a tiny Texas town. It was a tough time for Alvin's family and for lots of Americans. There wasn't enough money or jobs to go around. But Alvin's mom worked hard to provide for him. When Alvin was 12, he and his mom moved to Los Angeles, California.

While Alvin's mom worked, he went to theaters around the city. That's where he discovered dance! One day, on a class trip, he saw the Ballet Russe de Monte Carlo perform. From then on, Alvin was hooked. He started taking classes at the Lester Horton Dance Company.

DANCING TOGETHER

The Lester Horton Dance Company was one of the very first **integrated** dance companies. That means that anybody could dance there—no matter their race or ethnicity.

At first, Alvin didn't want to take dance seriously. He knew that Black dancers weren't always welcome in the biggest, best companies and theaters. And he knew that **LGBTQ** dancers, like himself, weren't welcome either.

Instead, Alvin took college courses in foreign languages. He was a great student. But still, Alvin's mind wandered to the arts—especially dance.

Alvin began to dance again. He watched his body move in the mirror. He was choreographing his own pieces. And he was good at it! In fact, Alvin was an excellent choreographer.

Alvin's **mentor**, Lester Horton, saw Alvin's talent. Then, in 1953, Lester passed away. Alvin was sad, but he was also brave. He was going to do something very challenging. He was going to become the **director** of the Lester Horton Dance Company!

Alvin was the director for one year. Then he moved to New York City. Alvin had an idea. A big idea.

He thought about it...
...he waited...
...and he finally decided to create his own dance company in New York City!

And this company would have his own name: Alvin Ailey American Dance Theater (AAADT).

Alvin wanted his theater to be a home for all kinds of dancers. He wanted it to be one of the top modern dance companies. He also wanted his theater to shine a spotlight on Black dancers and dances. Alvin's theater would tell important stories of history and **heritage**.

PLAYBILL
AAADT

ALVIN AILEY

MERICAN
ANCE
HEATER

That theater was just the first step of Alvin's journey. In the years that followed, he choreographed 79 original works. His most popular piece, *Revelations*, was produced in 1960. Alvin designed the dance to speak to everyone. It explored African American spirituals, blues, and gospel music. Some parts of *Revelations* were very sad. Other parts were full of joy. The dance had both—just like life.

COMING OUT

Alvin kept one part of his life very private. While some people choose to **come out**, others don't. Alvin never did. This is sometimes called being closeted.

Alvin also wrote a ballet called *Cry*. He created it as a birthday present for his mom. His **muse** for the dance was Judith Jamison. She was a star at the AAADT and performed the ballet. They dedicated it to Black women everywhere, especially moms.

Alvin traveled around the country with AAADT. Then the company traveled around the world. The AAADT has performed in over 70 countries. Fans lined up to see the moving ballets and modern dances. In 1988, Alvin received the Kennedy Center Honor for an entire lifetime of achievement.

At just 58 years old, Alvin lost his life to complications from HIV/AIDS. In the 1980s, this disease hurt and killed many people in the LGBTQ community.

Alvin's company continues his work to this day. In 2014, 25 years after his death, Alvin was awarded the Presidential Medal of Freedom. He had brought dance to new audiences. Through hard work and determination, Alvin helped show the world something beautiful: that dance was for everybody, everywhere.

> **Dance is for everybody. I believe that the dance came from the people and that it should always be delivered back to the people.**
> –Alvin Ailey

TIME LINE

1931 Alvin Ailey Jr. is born to Alvin Ailey and Lula Elizabeth Ailey in Rogers, Texas.

1949 Alvin gets involved with the Lester Horton Dance Theater in Los Angeles, California.

1953 Lester Horton passes away, and Alvin becomes the artistic director at the Lester Horton Dance Theater.

1958 Alvin and a group of modern dancers perform for the very first time as members of Alvin Ailey American Dance Theater in New York City.

1960 Alvin choreographs *Revelations*, which will later be known as his masterpiece.

1969 Alvin opens a dance school. Today it is known as The Ailey School.

1971 Alvin choreographs *Cry* for his mother as a birthday present.

1974 Seeking to support young artists, Alvin establishes the Alvin Ailey Repertory Ensemble, now known as Ailey II.

1988 Alvin receives the Kennedy Center Honor for a lifetime of achievement.

1989 Alvin establishes AileyCamp, a free dance day camp for kids ages 11 to 14.

1989 Alvin passes away from AIDS-related complications.

2014 Twenty-five years after Alvin's death, President Obama awards him the Presidential Medal of Freedom.

GLOSSARY

choreographer (kor-ee-AH-gruh-fur): a person who arranges steps and movements for a dance

come out (kuhm out): to openly announce one's sexual orientation or gender identity

director (duh-REK-tur): someone who is in charge of important decisions for a company or organization

heritage (HER-i-tij): traditions and beliefs that a society or group considers an important part of its history

integrated (IN-ti-grate-id): to have included people of all races and ethnicities

LGBTQ (ell-gee-bee-tee-queue): lesbian, gay, bisexual, transgender, and queer/questioning

mentor (MEN-tor): someone who helps, teaches, or gives advice to someone less experienced

muse (myooz): a person or thing, real or imaginary, that serves as an inspiration to an artist

INDEX

Alvin Ailey American Dance Theater 14, 18, 19

choreographing 12

Lester Horton 8, 9, 12

Los Angeles 6

music 5, 16

New York City 14

Judith Jamison 18

student 10

TEXT-DEPENDENT QUESTIONS

1. Who was Alvin's mentor?
2. What did Alvin believe about dance?
3. What does a choreographer do?
4. Why did Alvin study foreign languages instead of dance?
5. How did Alvin discover dance?

EXTENSION ACTIVITY

Alvin Ailey was a choreographer. That means he made up dances for himself and for other dancers! Now's your chance to step into the spotlight as the dancer and choreographer–just like Alvin! First, find your favorite song. Listen to the rhythm and the tune. Move your body to the music. Then, write down the steps to your dance. Finally, try teaching your dance to someone else, or performing it for your friends or family members.

ABOUT THE AUTHOR

Kaitlyn Duling believes in the power of self-expression, whether that means dancing your socks off or writing until your fingers ache. Kaitlyn grew up in Illinois, but now lives with her wife in Washington, DC. She has written more than 100 books for children and teens. She hopes her books will inspire readers to live in their truth and to dance like no one is watching.

ABOUT THE ILLUSTRATOR

Arvilla Mae Morett is an illustrator and artist focused on feminism, mental health, and animal rights. She loves exploring new mediums such as watercolor and gouache. Her adventurous spirit allows her to express ideas and educate through illustrations. When she isn't creating, you can find her spending time with her family or helping foster dogs.

www.rourkebooks.com

PHOTO CREDITS: cover, page 1: Illustration based on photograph by Normand Maxon. Courtesy of the Alvin Ailey Dance Foundation Archives. page 20: Collection of the Smithsonian National Museum of African American History and Culture and Alvin Ailey Dance Foundation, Inc., Photograph by Jack Mitchell, © Alvin Ailey Dance Foundation, Inc. and Smithsonian Institution, All rights reserved.

Quote source: Kindra Becker-Redd and Michael Magilligan "Alvin Ailey & Fordham: Innovation in Collaboration" Fordham Library News, March 11, 2021, https://librarynews.blog.fordham.edu/2021/03/11/alvin-ailey-and-fordham/

Edited by: Hailey Scragg
Illustrations by: Arvilla Mae Morett
Cover and interior layout by: J.J. Giddings

Library of Congress PCN Data

Alvin Ailey / Kaitlyn Duling
(Leaders Like Us)
ISBN 978-1-73165-281-2 (hard cover)
ISBN 978-1-73165-251-5 (soft cover)
ISBN 978-1-73165-311-6 (e-book)
ISBN 978-1-73165-341-3 (e-pub)
Library of Congress Control Number: 2021952167

Rourke Educational Media
Printed in the United States of America
01-2412211937